WILDERNESS NAVIGATION FOR BEGINNERS

The Ultimate Guide on Finding your Bearings Maximizing Map and Compass During Wilderness Trips Including Navigational Skills for Hikers and Survivalist

Mina Mong
Copyright@2024

TABLE OF CONTENT

CHAPTER 1

INTRODUCTION

The Significance of Navigating in Wilderness Adventures

Exploring the great outdoors provides an unmatched feeling of liberation and excitement. Many are drawn to the tranquil allure of pristine landscapes, the excitement of venturing into unknown territories, and the sense of accomplishment that comes with relying on oneself in outdoor pursuits like hiking and survival expeditions. However, the sense of freedom that comes with exploring the great outdoors also carries the potential danger of losing your way, transforming what should be an exciting adventure into a potentially dangerous predicament. Here is where the art of navigation becomes not just a handy skill, but a crucial one for those venturing into remote or unfamiliar territories.

Effective navigation is crucial for ensuring a secure and prosperous journey through the wilderness. Without proper guidance, even the most seasoned adventurer can easily lose their way. Traversing the untamed and unfamiliar terrains of the great outdoors can be quite disorienting for the unprepared. Getting disoriented in unfamiliar territory can have serious repercussions, such as being exposed to extreme weather conditions, limited access to essential resources like food and water, and potentially life-threatening situations. Thus, becoming skilled in navigation techniques is essential for guaranteeing both the pleasure of the journey and the well-being and survival of the traveler.

 Introduction to the Map and Compass as Crucial Tools

When it comes to navigating in the wilderness, the map and compass are unmatched in their reliability and importance. In contrast to modern GPS devices, which depend on batteries and satellite signals that may fail or become unreachable, a map and compass are completely self-reliant. Their method of navigation has stood the test of time and is known for its reliability, having been utilized for centuries.

A map, especially a topographic map, provides a comprehensive depiction of the landscape, encompassing natural elements like mountains, valleys, and rivers, as well as human-made elements like trails and roads. It enables hikers and survivalists to gain a comprehensive understanding of the terrain, strategize their routes, and determine their precise position in relation to familiar landmarks.

On the other hand, a compass is a straightforward yet effective tool that indicates the direction in relation to the Earth's magnetic poles. When combined with a map, a compass becomes an invaluable tool for determining precise bearings, allowing travelers to navigate with utmost accuracy between different points. With a solid grasp of map reading and compass interpretation, individuals can confidently and accurately navigate through the wilderness.

 Advantages for Outdoor Enthusiasts and Those with a Knack for Survival

There are numerous advantages to becoming skilled in map and compass navigation that go beyond simply preventing oneself from becoming lost. These abilities provide hikers and survivalists with a range of important benefits:

1. Increased Safety and Confidence: Having the ability to navigate through unfamiliar terrain using a map and compass provides a comforting sense of assurance. Adventurers can fearlessly

venture into uncharted territories, assured of their ability to navigate their way back. In emergency situations, being able to find a known location or determine the fastest route to safety can be crucial for saving lives.

2. Increased Self-Reliance: - Depending too heavily on electronic devices for navigation can be dangerous in the wilderness. It's always a possibility for batteries to run out, devices to malfunction, and signals to disappear. Armed with a map and compass, adventurers and outdoor enthusiasts gain the ability to navigate independently, relying solely on their own skills rather than modern technology.

3. A Stronger Bond with the Surroundings: Successfully navigating through unfamiliar landscapes demands a deep familiarity with the surrounding environment. This practice promotes a heightened awareness of one's surroundings, fostering a stronger bond with the natural world. It improves your understanding of your surroundings and helps you develop a deeper connection with nature.

4. Enhanced Planning and Preparation: - Utilizing a map and compass enables more thorough trip planning. Plotting

routes for hikers involves considering elevation changes, potential obstacles, and points of interest along the way. Being well-prepared ensures that your journeys are more enjoyable and efficient.

5. Skill Development: - Mastering the art of navigation using a map and compass enhances critical thinking and problem-solving abilities. One must interpret data, make decisions based on limited information, and adapt to changing conditions. These skills have immense value, not just in the great outdoors, but also in our day-to-day lives.

6. Cultural and Historical Appreciation: - The methods of navigating using maps and compasses have a fascinating and storied past. Grasping these techniques links present-day adventurers to the pioneers of yesteryear, fostering a feeling of ongoing legacy and admiration for the customs of exploration and resilience.

7. Environmental Stewardship: - Traveling without relying on marked trails or electronic devices encourages travelers to practice Leave No Trace principles more effectively. It emphasizes the importance of preserving the environment by encouraging individuals

to avoid creating new paths and disturbing wildlife.

8. Rescue and Assistance: - When hikers or survivalists encounter individuals in need of help, their dependable navigational skills allow them to provide precise directions, lead rescue operations, or assist emergency services in finding the precise location, potentially making a life-saving difference.

9. Adaptability in Different Environments: Having a strong understanding of map and compass skills is crucial even in challenging situations. They excel in a wide range of environments, from thick forests to rugged mountains and arid deserts. Their versatility makes them essential for any adventurer exploring the great outdoors.

10. Increased Pleasure in the Great Outdoors: - Ultimately, having a strong sense of direction and navigation skills greatly enhances the overall enjoyment of exploring the great outdoors. Exploring uncharted territories, uncovering hidden treasures, and venturing into remote areas brings an extra dose of excitement and satisfaction to the expedition.

Navigation is absolutely crucial when

embarking on wilderness trips. The map and compass remain steadfast and dependable, offering hikers and survivalists the means to navigate with confidence and efficiency. Developing proficiency in these abilities not only increases safety and self-assurance, but also cultivates a stronger bond with nature, encourages self-reliance, and enhances the overall adventure in the great outdoors. In a world where technology is constantly evolving, the timeless skills of map and compass navigation remain crucial. These skills provide the necessary knowledge and confidence for those who explore the great outdoors, allowing them to thrive in the wilderness.

CHAPTER 2

Understanding Maps

Successfully navigating through the wilderness requires a strong skill in deciphering and understanding maps. Maps offer a visual depiction of a region, showcasing the lay of the land, notable landmarks, and other important elements. For those venturing into the great outdoors, having a solid grasp of various map types and the ability to decipher their symbols is essential for navigating with confidence.

A. Different Kinds of Maps

There are different types of maps, each with its own purpose. These are the main types of maps that are important for navigating in the wilderness:

1. Topographic Maps - Description: Topographic maps provide intricate depictions of the Earth's terrain, showcasing both natural wonders and human-made structures. Contour lines are included to show elevation changes, which makes them perfect for getting a grasp on the lay of the land.
   - Uses: These maps are crucial for individuals who venture into the great

outdoors, whether it be for hiking, climbing, or survival purposes. They offer a comprehensive and detailed representation of the terrain, allowing for better navigation and understanding of the surroundings. They assist in route planning, assessing terrain challenges, and recognizing potential obstacles.

2. Road Maps - Description: Road maps provide detailed information about roads, highways, and major transportation routes. They frequently incorporate towns, cities, and points of interest, but they do not provide extensive topographic details.
   - Uses: Road maps can be helpful for planning the journey to and from the wilderness area, although they may not be the best option for navigating deep within the wilderness. They can also come in handy for locating nearby facilities, like gas stations or hospitals.

3. Specialty Maps (e.g., Orienteering) - Description: Specialty maps are designed for specific activities. Maps used for orienteering, for instance, are incredibly intricate and specifically created for the activity. They highlight key elements for effective navigation, including different types of vegetation, distinctive rock formations, and detailed contours.

- Uses: These maps are perfect for recreational activities that require precise navigation, such as orienteering. They are also great for thoroughly exploring smaller sections of the wilderness.

B. Understanding Map Reading

Having a solid grasp of a map's symbols, contours, and scales is crucial for effective navigation.

1. Understanding Map Symbols and Legend - Description: Maps utilize a wide range of symbols to depict various elements, including rivers, trails, buildings, and vegetation. A common feature on maps is the legend, which provides explanations for the various symbols used.
   - Significance: Being knowledgeable about these symbols enables hikers and survivalists to swiftly recognize crucial features and landmarks. For example, having knowledge of the symbols for water sources or shelters can be crucial in survival situations.

2. Contour Lines and Elevation - Explanation: Contour lines on topographic maps provide information about elevation. The different lines on the map indicate different elevations, while the spacing between them

indicates the steepness of the terrain. Observing the spacing between lines can provide insights into the terrain's steepness. If the lines are closely spaced, it indicates steep slopes, whereas widely spaced lines suggest more gentle slopes.

   - Importance: Having a good grasp of contour lines is crucial when it comes to evaluating the challenges posed by the landscape and strategizing your navigation. Through the interpretation of contour lines, experienced navigators are able to navigate through the terrain with ease, avoiding difficult uphill climbs or treacherous descents, and finding the most convenient routes.

3. Scale and Distance - Description: The scale of a map illustrates the correlation between distances on the map and real-life distances on the ground. Typically, it is represented as a ratio, such as 1:25,000, indicating that 1 unit on the map corresponds to 25,000 units in reality.

   - Significance: Understanding how to utilize the scale is crucial for accurately estimating distances and effectively planning travel time between different locations. It is essential to effectively manage resources and ensure timely arrival at destinations.

C. Understanding Map Orientation

After gaining a grasp on map reading, the subsequent task involves aligning it accurately with the surrounding landscape.

1. Map Alignment with the Terrain - Description: Positioning the map in a way that matches the actual features in front of you. Typically, one would use a compass to make sure that the map's north is correctly aligned with true north.
   - Instructions:
   1. Locate a familiar point of reference: Discover a distinguishable landmark both on the map and in the surrounding terrain.
   2. Adjust the map: Rotate the map until the landmark on the map lines up with the actual landmark.
   3. Utilize a compass: Position the compass on the map, making sure the compass needle aligns with the map's north. Make the necessary adjustments to the map.
   - Significance: Having a good understanding of map orientation is crucial for precise navigation. It guarantees that the paths you follow on the map align perfectly with the actual paths in the terrain.

2. Using Landmarks for Orientation - Description: Landmarks are distinctive features in the surroundings that are

easily identifiable, such as mountains, rivers, or man-made structures.
   - Instructions:
   1. Observe notable features: Take note of prominent landmarks in your surroundings and find them on the map.
   2. Utilize various landmarks to determine your position by drawing lines from these landmarks and identifying their intersection on the map.
   3. Continuously update your position by identifying new landmarks and repeating the process as you move.
   - Significance: Utilizing landmarks as a means of orientation offers a dependable approach to keeping track of your direction and confirming your location. This technique is particularly handy in situations where visibility is restricted or when maneuvering through intricate landscapes.

Having a solid grasp of maps is essential for individuals who enjoy exploring the great outdoors. Having a good understanding of various maps and their specific purposes is essential for ensuring you have the appropriate tool for your outdoor escapades. Understanding a map requires the ability to decipher symbols, contour lines, and scales, all of which offer valuable insights into the landscape and distances. Mastering the art of map orientation, compass usage, and landmark identification is crucial for accurate navigation and ensuring safety and confidence in the great outdoors.

Developing proficiency in these skills not only equips you to tackle navigation obstacles effectively, but also cultivates a stronger bond with nature and a heightened admiration for the intricacies of map-making. Armed with a wealth of knowledge from your map and a trusty compass, you can fearlessly venture into the great outdoors, ensuring your expeditions are both secure and delightful.

CHAPTER 3

Mastering the Compass

Having a solid understanding of how to use a compass is crucial for successful navigation in the great outdoors. Understanding how to properly utilize a compass is essential for successfully navigating through various landscapes. In this section, we will explore the different parts and varieties of compasses, along with the methods for effectively utilizing a compass. This includes acquiring and tracking a bearing, as well as making adjustments for declination.

 A. Parts of a Compass

Having a solid grasp of the components of a compass is essential for its optimal functionality. These are the essential elements:

1. Baseplate - Description: The baseplate is a flat, transparent surface that serves as the foundation for the compass. It frequently incorporates rulers and scales for measuring distances on maps.
   - Functions:

1. The baseplate's straight edges and rulers assist in aligning the compass with map features.

2. This tool offers a reliable platform for establishing and tracking directions.

3. Rulers and scales are essential tools for measuring distances on maps, which greatly improve accuracy when planning routes.

- Significance: A carefully crafted baseplate improves the accuracy of map work and boosts the overall effectiveness of the compass.

2. Arrow indicating direction of travel - Description: There is a direction-of-travel arrow on the baseplate that shows you which way to go.

- Functions:

1. Proper alignment: When taking a bearing, make sure to align the arrow with the direction you want to go.

2. Navigation: It indicates the direction that should be followed after setting a bearing.

- Significance: This arrow plays a crucial role in converting bearings into practical movement on the terrain, guaranteeing that you remain on the right path.

3. Rotating Bezel (or Azimuth Ring) - Description: The rotating bezel is a circular, movable ring marked with

degrees (0° to 360°) surrounding the compass needle.
   - Functions:
   1. Setting bearings: Adjust the bezel to align with the magnetic needle to establish a bearing.
   2. Measurement: This feature enables accurate measurement and adjustment of angles.
   - Significance: The bezel plays a vital role in precisely adjusting and interpreting bearings, which are essential for navigation.

4. Magnetic Needle - Description: The magnetic needle is a magnetized pointer that aligns itself with the Earth's magnetic field, indicating the direction of north.
   - Functions:
   1. Orientation: It offers a dependable indication of magnetic north.
   2. The alignment of the needle with the bezel ensures precise bearing settings.
   - Significance: The magnetic needle serves as the core component of the compass, offering the essential directional reference required for navigation.

  B. Different Types of Compasses

There are a variety of compasses available to meet different navigational requirements. These are the main types:

1. Baseplate Compass - Description: A baseplate compass has a clear baseplate with a magnetic needle and a rotating bezel. It is specifically designed for navigation using maps.
   - Characteristics:
     1. The baseplate is transparent, making map reading a breeze.
     2. Tools for measurement and map alignment: Assist in determining distances and ensuring accurate map placement.
     3. Certain models offer the convenience of an adjustable declination feature, allowing for easy correction of magnetic declination.
   - Usage: Perfect for hikers and outdoor enthusiasts who depend on precise maps for finding their way.
   - Significance: The baseplate compass holds great value due to its versatility and user-friendly nature, which has led to its widespread use in wilderness navigation.

2. Lensatic Compass - Description: The lensatic compass is a popular choice among military personnel due to its sighting lens, which allows for accurate bearings.

- Characteristics:
    1. Sighting lens: Improves precision in determining bearings by enabling direct sighting of landmarks.
    2. The folding cover serves a dual purpose - it keeps the compass safe and can also be utilized for sighting.
    3. Glow-in-the-dark markings: Help with navigating in the dark.
    - Usage: Ideal for situations that demand exceptional accuracy, such as military operations and professional surveying.
    - Significance: The lensatic compass offers enhanced precision when determining bearings over extensive distances, making it an invaluable tool in situations that require precise navigation.

C. Utilizing a Compass

Mastering the art of compass navigation requires a deep understanding of various techniques, all of which play a vital role in ensuring successful navigation. These are the main techniques:

1. Finding Your Way - Description: Finding your way involves determining the direction from your current location to a distant point.
    - Instructions:

1. Choose a target: Select a prominent landmark or feature on the map to navigate towards.

2. Hold the compass flat and point the direction-of-travel arrow towards the target to align it.

3. Adjust the bezel: Rotate the bezel until the magnetic needle lines up with the orienting arrow, which indicates north.

4. Determine the bearing: The number indicated by the direction-of-travel arrow on the bezel represents your current bearing.

- Significance: Ensuring an accurate bearing is crucial in order to accurately navigate towards your desired destination.

2. Navigating through the Wilderness - Description: Moving in the direction set by the bearing is an essential skill for navigating through the wilderness.

- Instructions:

1. Determine the direction: Follow the steps provided to accurately determine the direction.

2. Ensure proper compass handling: Maintain a flat position for the compass, holding it in front of you.

3. Keep the magnetic needle aligned with the orienting arrow as you move.

4. Proceed towards the desired destination: Follow the direction shown

by the arrow and regularly confirm that the needle remains in line.

   - Significance: Maintaining a precise direction ensures that you stay on the right track, avoiding any detours or possible confusion.

3. Adjusting for Declination - Description: Declination refers to the angle variation between magnetic north (as shown by the compass needle) and true north (geographic north). Ensuring accurate navigation requires adjusting for declination.

   - Instructions:

   1. Find the local declination: Get the current declination value for your location from a map or online source.

   2. Make sure to adjust the compass if it has a declination adjustment mechanism. Set it to the correct angle for accurate navigation. Alternatively, you can manually adjust your bearings.

      - When dealing with east declination, it's important to remember to include the declination value in your bearing.

      - To account for west declination, simply subtract the declination value from your bearing.

   3. Set the adjusted bearing: Follow the steps to determine a bearing, and then make the necessary adjustments for declination before proceeding.

   - Significance: Taking into account declination helps to eliminate any inaccuracies that may arise from the variation between magnetic and true north, thus ensuring accurate navigation.

 Real-Life Use of Compass Skills

To gain a deeper understanding of how these compass skills can be applied, let's explore a few different scenarios:

Scenario 1: Navigating Through Dense Forest - Challenge: Finding your way through a dense forest where landmarks are nowhere to be seen.
- Solution:
  - Find Your Direction: Before venturing into the forest, make sure to locate a distant target and determine your direction.
  - Stay on Course: Utilize the compass to stay on track, making sure the needle remains in line with the orienting arrow.
  - Take into Account Declination: Make sure to adjust the bearing to account for the local declination.
  - Utilize Natural Features: Take advantage of the surrounding environment, such as streams or ridges, to help guide your way.

Scenario 2: Night Navigation Using a Compass - Challenge: Finding your way in the dark with limited visibility.
- Solution: - Utilize a Headlamp: Make sure to have a headlamp equipped with a red light to maintain your night vision.
  - Establish a Direction: Utilize the compass to establish a direction by aligning it with a prominent star or celestial body.
  - Stay on course: Follow the direction shown by the arrow and regularly use the compass to ensure you stay on track.

Scenario 3: Navigating in Adverse Weather - Challenge: Navigating in challenging weather conditions with limited visibility due to fog or heavy rain.
- Solution: - Set a Direction: Establish a course towards a familiar location before visibility decreases.
  - Stay on Track: Utilize the compass to maintain your direction, regularly verifying that you're on the right path.
  - Account for Declination: Take into consideration the local declination to ensure precise direction.
  - Estimating Distances: Utilize pacing to gauge the distances covered, especially when visual cues are not easily visible.

Having a strong grasp of compass usage is an essential skill for individuals venturing into the great outdoors. Having a good grasp of the different parts of a compass is essential for using it effectively. Understanding different types of compasses, such as baseplate and lensatic compasses, helps in selecting the most suitable tool for your requirements.

Mastering the art of compass navigation requires precision in determining bearings, diligently following those bearings, and making necessary adjustments to account for the variation between magnetic and true north. Applying these skills in real-life situations guarantees precise and dependable navigation in a range of scenarios, including traversing thick forests, navigating at night, or dealing with challenging weather conditions.

Through a deep understanding of compass skills, individuals who venture into the great outdoors can navigate with confidence and security. This knowledge not only enhances their outdoor experiences but also guarantees their ability to find their way in any type of environment.

CHAPTER 4

Integrating Map and Compass

Mastering the art of map reading and compass usage is crucial for accurate navigation in the great outdoors. When these tools are used together, hikers and survivalists can navigate more accurately and confidently. In this section, we delve into the art of navigating through the great outdoors. We will discuss the methods of triangulation, planning your route, and employing different strategies to find your way using a combination of maps and compasses.

A. Triangulation

Triangulation is a technique that allows you to pinpoint your precise location by using bearings to reference two familiar landmarks and marking their positions on a map. This technique is extremely useful when you find yourself uncertain of your location in the great outdoors.

1. Identifying Landmarks - Description: The initial stage of triangulation involves recognizing and noting significant and easily identifiable elements in the surrounding environment, such as

towering mountains, structures, or other unique landmarks.

   - Instructions:

   1. Observe your surroundings: Keep a keen eye on the surroundings, searching for distinct landmarks that match both the terrain and your map.

   2. Verify the landmarks on the map: Find these features on your map, making sure they are clearly marked and easy to recognize.

   3. Choose several points of interest: Select a minimum of two, ideally three, landmarks that are well spread out to ensure greater precision.

   - Significance: Precise recognition of landmarks plays a vital role in achieving accurate triangulation. Confusing one landmark with another can result in major mistakes when determining your location.

2. Plotting Positions on the Map - Description: After identifying the landmarks, you can determine your position by taking bearings to these landmarks and drawing lines on your map.

   - Instructions:

   1. Use your compass to determine the direction to the first landmark. Align the direction-of-travel arrow with the landmark and adjust the bezel until the

magnetic needle lines up with the orienting arrow.

    2. Draw a line: On your map, place the compass on the landmark and carefully trace a line along the edge of the compass in the direction you want to go.

    3. Continue with additional landmarks: Determine the bearings to the second and third landmarks, and then plot lines from these points on the map.

    4. Find your position: Your location is determined by the point where the lines intersect.

  - Significance: Accurately plotting positions enables you to precisely determine your location on the map. Understanding your current location and strategizing for the next leg of your adventure is of utmost importance.

B. Planning Your Route

Efficient route planning is crucial for a triumphant adventure in the great outdoors. By carefully marking key locations and accurately measuring distances, you can ensure a smooth and successful journey.

1. Setting Waypoints - Description: Waypoints are designated spots on your map that help you navigate your desired path.

- Instructions:
  1. Identify important locations: On your map, mark important locations along your route, such as where trails intersect, where you can find water, and where you can set up camp.
  2. Make sure to mark waypoints on your map by using symbols or notes.
  3. Chart your course: Connect the waypoints with lines to map out your desired route.
  4. Determine the direction for each segment of the route between waypoints by using your compass to set the bearings.
- Significance: Establishing waypoints is crucial for dividing a lengthy expedition into manageable sections, enhancing navigation by providing structure and order. It also enables more effective monitoring of progress and timely adjustments.

2. Measuring Distances - Description: Calculating the distances between waypoints is crucial for estimating travel time and effectively managing resources such as food and water.
  - Instructions:
  1. Utilize the map scale: Determine the scale of your map (e.g., 1:25,000) and make use of the ruler on the baseplate of your compass or a separate scale tool.

2. Measure distance: Align the ruler or compass along the path connecting two waypoints and determine the distance.

3. Calculate the actual distance: Utilize the scale on the map to determine the distance in real-world measurements, such as kilometers or miles.

4. Determine travel time: Use your average hiking speed to estimate how long it will take to travel each segment.

- Importance: Precise distance measurement is crucial for efficient time management and ensuring you have enough resources for your expedition. It also assists in establishing attainable daily travel objectives.

C. Navigational Techniques

Mastering certain techniques can greatly improve your ability to navigate through unfamiliar terrain and successfully navigate around potential obstacles. Strategies such as aiming off, utilizing handrails, and identifying key landmarks are especially valuable when navigating through difficult terrain.

1. Aiming Off - Description: Aiming off is a technique that can help you reach a specific point, like a trail junction or river crossing, even if your bearing is slightly off.

- Instructions:
    1. Identify the destination: Determine the specific location you need to reach, such as a trail or river.
    2. Set a slightly offset bearing instead of a direct one to the feature.
    3. Find your way: Continue in the direction until you come across the desired landmark.
    4. Change direction and track the feature: Once you arrive at the feature, adjust your direction accordingly and track it until you reach your destination.
    - Significance: Aiming off is crucial in order to avoid missing your destination as a result of small navigation mistakes. This is especially helpful when finding your way to linear features such as trails or rivers that are easy to follow once you reach them.

2. Handrails and Catching Features - Description: Handrails are linear features in the landscape that can be followed, such as rivers, ridges, or roads. Notable landmarks can serve as indicators that you have exceeded your intended destination, such as a prominent hill or a sizable body of water.
    - Instructions:
    1. Locate handrails: Search for noticeable linear features on your map that run alongside your planned path.

2. Utilize handrails: Navigate by following these features, using them as guides.

3. Recognize key landmarks: Note important landmarks on your map that signal the need to pause or alter your course.

4. Stay vigilant: While journeying, be sure to watch for these landmarks to confirm you're headed in the correct direction and to prevent going past your intended destination.

- Significance: Utilizing handrails and identifiable landmarks simplifies navigation by offering distinct physical guides and boundaries. This method is useful for avoiding getting disoriented and guarantees that you can adjust your path if needed.

Mastering the art of map reading and compass usage is crucial for successfully navigating through the wilderness. By mastering techniques such as triangulation, route planning, and employing navigational strategies like aiming off and using handrails and catching features, hikers and survivalists can navigate the wilderness with precision and confidence. By honing these essential abilities, you can confidently navigate through untamed landscapes, efficiently utilize available resources, and fully savor the thrill of your outdoor escapades.

Having the skill to accurately pinpoint your whereabouts, strategize efficient paths, and utilize effective navigation methods guarantees your ability to tackle a range of scenarios in the great outdoors. Mastering these skills will enhance your ability to navigate in the great outdoors, ensuring your safety and self-sufficiency. This will ultimately make your adventures in nature more fulfilling and less anxiety-inducing.

CHAPTER 5

Advanced Navigational Skills

For those who are experienced in outdoor exploration or survival, it is crucial to acquire advanced navigational abilities in order to successfully navigate intricate landscapes and guarantee safety in demanding surroundings. These skills extend beyond the fundamentals of map and compass usage, incorporating techniques like dead reckoning, relying on natural indicators, and combining GPS technology with traditional navigation methods. This section offers a complete guide to these advanced skills.

 A. Navigating through the Unknown

Dead reckoning is a method of navigation that requires you to determine your current position using a previously known position, and then make educated guesses about the direction, distance, and speed you have traveled. It can be especially handy in situations with limited visibility, like dense forests or inclement weather.

1. Estimating Distances - Description: Precise distance estimation is essential for accurate dead reckoning. One way to

determine your distance traveled is by calculating it using your speed and time, or by relying on familiar landmarks and pacing.

- Instructions:

1. Pacing: Measure your steps over a familiar distance to calculate your typical stride length. As an illustration, if it requires 66 steps to cover a distance of 100 meters, your stride length would be 1.5 meters.

2. Time estimation: By having knowledge of your typical walking speed (e.g., 5 km/h), it becomes possible to make an estimation of the distance covered within a certain timeframe. After walking for 2 hours at a steady pace of 5 km/h, you would have traveled a distance of around 10 kilometers.

3. Estimating distances using landmarks on your map can be quite helpful. If a familiar point of reference is 3 kilometers away on the map and you arrive there in 30 minutes, your speed is 6 km/h.

- Significance: Precise distance estimation plays a crucial role in ensuring an exact position fix, particularly in situations where other navigation aids are not accessible.

2. Staying on Track - Description: Staying on track involves ensuring a consistent direction while traveling. It is

crucial to ensure that you stay on course and successfully reach your desired location.
   - Instructions:
   1. Establish a direction: Utilize your compass to determine the direction from your current location to your next waypoint.
   2. Stay on course: Follow the given direction and regularly use your compass to stay on track.
   3. Utilize reference points: Take note of the natural or man-made features along your route to assist in maintaining your course. For instance, set your sights on a tree or hill in the distance that lines up with the direction you want to go.
   4. Make adjustments for any deviations: If you happen to veer off course, simply correct your direction to get back on track. Make sure to consistently monitor your compass and the environment around you to stay on track.
   - Significance: Maintaining a steady course is crucial for avoiding unnecessary diversions and ensuring efficient travel, which in turn minimizes the chances of becoming disoriented.

B. Utilizing Natural Indicators

When lacking a map or compass, relying on natural indicators like the sun, stars, and environmental clues can be incredibly useful for navigation.

1. Sun and Stars - Description: The sun and stars are dependable celestial bodies that can assist in determining direction and time.
   - Instructions:
   1. Using celestial cues: Celestial bodies provide valuable guidance, with the sun rising in the east and setting in the west. During midday in the northern hemisphere, the general direction is towards the south. Shadows can also serve as a helpful guide: in the northern hemisphere, shadows will always point towards the north.
      - The Shadow Stick Method: Stick a vertical branch into the earth and use a rock to mark the end of its shadow. After waiting for 15-30 minutes, you can mark the new position of the shadow tip. Connect the two points with a line that stretches from the left to the right, with the initial mark on the left side.
   2. Using the stars: During nighttime, the North Star (Polaris) serves as a dependable guide to determine the direction of north in the northern hemisphere. Discovering its location involves identifying the Big Dipper constellation and connecting a line from the outer edge of the bowl to the adjacent bright star.

- The Southern Cross Method: In the southern hemisphere, the Southern Cross constellation indicates the direction of the south celestial pole. Imagine drawing a line through the center of the cross and extending it to the horizon.
  - Significance: Understanding the use of celestial bodies for navigation offers an alternative approach when conventional tools are not accessible or functional.

2. Environmental Clues - Description: The natural surroundings provide a range of hints that can assist with finding direction and navigating.
  - Instructions:
    1. Vegetation patterns: It is common for moss to grow on the side of trees that faces north in the northern hemisphere. However, the accuracy of this method can be affected by various local factors.
    2. Animal behavior: Animals often follow trails that lead to water sources. In the evening, birds frequently make their way towards bodies of water.
    3. Wind patterns can be useful in determining orientation. Many regions experience consistent seasonal wind patterns.
    4. Pay attention to the topographic features of the landscape, as valleys and ridges can provide valuable guidance for

your journey. Water naturally flows downhill, which means that tracing the path of a stream can often lead to discovering larger bodies of water or even human settlements.

   - Significance: Utilizing environmental cues boosts situational awareness and can offer additional navigational assistance in the absence of primary tools.

C. Integration with GPS

GPS devices offer accurate location information by utilizing satellite technology. Combining GPS with traditional navigation methods brings together the precision of modern technology with the dependability of timeless tools.

1. Advantages and Disadvantages - Advantages:
   1. Precision: GPS devices have the ability to determine your precise location with a high level of accuracy.
   2. Convenience: GPS units are user-friendly and can swiftly provide directions, distances, and routes.
   3. GPS devices have the capability to store waypoints, routes, and tracks, making navigation and trip planning a breeze.
   - Downsides:

1. Reliance on batteries: GPS units require batteries, which can deplete, leaving you without navigation.

2. Signal issues: Dense forests, deep valleys, and other obstacles may interfere with GPS signals, resulting in decreased accuracy or signal loss.

3. Dependability: Electronic devices may experience malfunctions or damage, rendering them less reliable in challenging environments.

- Significance: Having a clear understanding of the advantages and disadvantages of GPS devices is crucial for making well-informed choices regarding their usage and being prepared with alternative navigation methods.

2. Enhancing Navigation with a Blend of Modern and Traditional Techniques - Description: By combining the accuracy of GPS technology with the tried-and-true methods of map reading and compass navigation, one can greatly improve their overall effectiveness in finding their way.

- Instructions:

1. Confirm GPS data: Compare GPS coordinates with your map to ensure accuracy. Utilize the GPS to determine your precise whereabouts and subsequently pinpoint it on the map.

2. Enter waypoints: Input the coordinates from your map into the GPS for convenient navigation. This enables you to navigate pre-determined routes with greater accuracy.

3. Use as a backup: Place your trust in the map and compass as your primary tools, utilizing the GPS only as a secondary option or for confirming your location. Even if the GPS malfunctions, you can rely on your tried-and-true navigation techniques.

4. Keep an eye on battery life: Preserve battery power by disabling the GPS when it's not needed or by using it only when necessary.

5. Utilize a variety of techniques to enhance your navigation skills. Incorporate traditional methods such as triangulation and dead reckoning in conjunction with GPS data to achieve more precise results. For instance, utilize GPS to establish an initial direction and subsequently rely on the compass to track it.

- Significance: By integrating GPS technology with conventional methods, a holistic navigation approach is achieved, capitalizing on the unique advantages of each technology to guarantee precise and dependable results in diverse environments.

Final Thoughts

Having a strong grasp of navigation is crucial when it comes to successfully traversing difficult landscapes and ensuring your safety during outdoor expeditions. Methods like dead reckoning, utilizing natural cues, and combining GPS technology with traditional techniques offer a strong foundation for successful navigation.

Dead reckoning requires making estimations of distances and staying on track using a position that was determined earlier. Having this skill is extremely important in situations where visibility is limited or when other means of navigation are not accessible. Through precise distance estimation and unwavering adherence to a predetermined route, individuals exploring the great outdoors can ensure they stay on track and arrive at their desired destinations without any mishaps.

Utilizing natural indicators like the sun, stars, and environmental cues can offer valuable navigational assistance in situations where conventional tools are unavailable. Having a grasp of celestial bodies and being able to interpret environmental signs can greatly improve your situational awareness and provide dependable ways to figure out your direction and orientation.

Combining GPS technology with traditional navigation methods brings together the accuracy of modern devices with the dependability of timeless tools. Through the careful utilization of GPS data, maps, waypoints, and the GPS as a reliable backup, travelers can guarantee precise and streamlined navigation. Gaining a thorough understanding of the capabilities and constraints of GPS devices enables individuals to make well-informed decisions and be prepared with alternative navigation strategies.

Acquiring these advanced navigational skills empowers outdoor enthusiasts to confidently and securely venture into the untamed outdoors. Having a solid grasp of various navigation techniques, whether it's using GPS, maps and compasses, or relying on natural cues from the environment, is crucial for successful navigation in any scenario. Mastering these skills enhances the navigation experience and fosters self-sufficiency, adaptability, and the pure delight of exploring the great outdoors.

CHAPTER 6

Practical Applications and Scenarios

Having a strong grasp of navigational skills is essential for guaranteeing safety and achieving success during outdoor expeditions. This section delves into practical situations where these skills are crucial, including managing unexpected situations, finding your way in the dark, and adapting to challenging conditions like fog, thick forests, and unpredictable weather.

A. Stranded in the Wilderness

Discovering that you are lost in the wilderness can be a disorienting and frightening ordeal. Remaining composed and methodically readjusting your bearings is crucial for locating your path back to a secure location.

1. Keeping a Cool Head - Description: It's crucial to stay composed when you find yourself in an unfamiliar situation. Feeling overwhelmed can result in making hasty choices and making the situation worse.
   - Instructions:
     1. Cease: Promptly halt your movement to avoid further disorientation.

2. Reflect: Pause for a moment to gather your ideas and evaluate your circumstances.

3. Take a moment to carefully observe your surroundings. Look for any familiar landmarks or distinctive features that can help you navigate.

4. Strategy: Create a strategy by carefully considering your observations and the resources at your disposal.

- Reminder: Maintaining a calm demeanor enables you to think with clarity, make rational choices, and utilize your navigational tools to their fullest potential.

2. Finding Your Way - Description: Finding your way involves figuring out where you are and choosing the optimal path to safety.

- Instructions:

1. Utilize your map and compass: Attempt to determine your location by comparing your surroundings with the map.

2. Backtrack: If it's feasible, go back along the path you came from to a familiar spot. Keep an eye out for unique landmarks or indicators that you may have encountered before.

3. Determine your position: Utilize triangulation by taking bearings to familiar landmarks and marking them on your map to determine your location.

4. Determine a new direction: After determining your position, choose a new direction that leads to a familiar and secure location, like a campsite or a trailhead.

5. Call for assistance: If you find yourself unable to reorient, be ready to signal for help using a whistle, mirror, or by creating visible signals like a large SOS on the ground.

- Importance: Being able to effectively reorient yourself in the outdoors is crucial for ensuring your safety and minimizing the risk of prolonged exposure to the elements. It allows you to find your way back to safety or signal for rescue if needed.

B. Navigating in the Dark

Getting around in the dark can be quite tricky because it's hard to see where you're going. By utilizing specific techniques and keeping safety in mind, you can successfully navigate through various environments.

1. Strategies for Limited Visibility - Description: Moving through low visibility situations calls for different approaches to account for reduced sight.
- Instructions:

1. Utilize a headlamp: Opt for a headlamp that offers a red light option to

protect your night vision and allow for convenient hands-free lighting.

2. Utilize the stars: During clear nights, rely on constellations such as the North Star (Polaris) in the northern hemisphere to determine your direction.

3. Remember to place reflective markers on your path if you intend to retrace your steps. These tools can assist you in maintaining your course.

4. Utilize pace counting to measure distances in situations where landmarks may be less visible. Measure your steps to gauge the distance covered.

5. Pay attention to the sounds around you. In dense forests or fog, listen for the sound of flowing water or rustling leaves to help you navigate.

- Significance: These techniques are crucial for maintaining direction and ensuring safety when navigating in conditions with limited visibility.

2. Safety Considerations - Description: Ensuring safety is of utmost importance when navigating in the dark. Low visibility heightens the potential for accidents.

- Instructions:

1. Take it easy: Adopt a more measured and careful pace to prevent any mishaps or accidents.

2. Remember to stay on the trail and avoid straying off the designated path.

Exploring unfamiliar terrain in the dark can easily cause a loss of direction.

3. It's always a good idea to have someone with you when you're out exploring. Stay together and make sure to keep in constant communication.

4. Make sure to have signal devices on hand, such as a whistle, flashlight, and other signaling tools, in case you need to get the attention of others nearby.

5. Be aware of your capabilities: If the navigation becomes challenging or dangerous, it might be wise to establish a camp and wait until morning to proceed.

- Safety First: Following these safety considerations is crucial to reduce the chances of getting hurt and to help you navigate successfully in low-light conditions.

C. Challenging Circumstances

Successfully navigating through challenging environments like fog, dense forests, or unpredictable weather conditions demands the ability to adapt and possess extra skills to ensure one's orientation and safety.

1. Navigating in Fog or Heavy Forest - Description: Dense fog and thick forests

can make it difficult to find your way through, obscuring landmarks and trails.
   - Instructions:
   1. Utilize a compass: Place significant reliance on your compass to consistently maintain a specific bearing. When navigating through dense fog, it's important to always keep your compass in sight and regularly monitor your direction.
   2. Utilize pacing and timing to make accurate estimations of distances covered. This is especially handy in forests where there are few landmarks to rely on.
   3. Remember to mark your trail using environmentally-friendly markers or flagging tape to help you navigate through the wilderness. This can be useful for retracing your path if necessary.
   4. Stick to the path: Stick to natural features like rivers, ridges, or trails that can help you navigate, even in difficult conditions.
   5. Utilize GPS: If you have access to a GPS device, make use of it to keep track of your location. Make sure to frequently monitor your position and confirm that you are heading in the right direction.
   - Significance: These strategies are crucial for staying oriented and avoiding

getting lost in situations with limited visibility.

2. Dealing with Weather Changes - Description: Sudden shifts in weather can have an impact on navigation by changing the surroundings, making it harder to identify landmarks, and affecting the effectiveness of navigational tools.
   - Instructions:
   1. Stay updated on weather conditions: Keep yourself informed about weather forecasts before and during your trip. Make sure to have a barometer or portable weather radio on hand to stay updated.
   2. Seek refuge: In the event of extreme weather, locate or construct a shelter and remain there until conditions improve.
   3. Ensure the safety of your equipment by keeping your map and compass shielded from the elements and free from moisture. Ensure that your belongings are protected from water by utilizing waterproof cases or bags.
   4. Stay open to adjusting your route and be flexible with your plans. When faced with unfavorable weather conditions, it's important to adjust your route and seek out safer terrain.
   5. Dress in layers and bring necessary gear like rain jackets and

thermal blankets to handle temperature fluctuations.

   6. Familiarize yourself with potential safe zones and escape routes on your map prior to embarking on your journey. Be prepared to swiftly navigate through unfamiliar terrain if the weather takes a sudden turn.

   - Importance: Being able to adapt to weather changes is crucial for ensuring your safety and taking necessary precautions in the face of severe weather conditions.

Having a strong sense of direction and the ability to navigate is essential when facing different challenges in the great outdoors. When faced with challenging situations like being disoriented, traveling in the dark, or encountering difficult weather, having a strong grasp of advanced techniques is crucial for maintaining safety and maximizing efficiency.

When you find yourself in an unfamiliar location, it's important to remain calm and approach the situation with a systematic mindset. Utilizing maps, compasses, and natural indicators can help you get your bearings and find your way. When navigating at night, it's important to use specialized techniques to handle limited visibility and ensure your safety. Challenging circumstances such as fog, dense forests, and unpredictable weather require flexibility and readiness to navigate successfully.

Remaining composed and systematically readjusting one's bearings when disoriented can avert anxiety and aid in reestablishing direction. Mastering various techniques is essential for successfully navigating through unfamiliar terrain and ensuring a safe return.

Getting around in the dark calls for adjusting to limited visibility. By utilizing headlamps, reflective markers, and celestial navigation techniques, one can effectively stay on course in unfamiliar terrain. It is crucial to prioritize safety by taking precautions such as maintaining a moderate pace, sticking to designated paths, and ensuring you have a companion.

In challenging environments such as foggy areas and dense forests, it is crucial to depend on compasses, pacing, and natural landmarks to stay on course. Being prepared for unpredictable weather involves closely monitoring conditions, taking steps to safeguard equipment, making necessary adjustments to routes, and having a clear understanding of escape routes to prioritize safety.

Developing proficiency in these practical techniques improves your ability to navigate effectively and ensures your confidence and safety when exploring the great outdoors. When confronted with the difficulties of losing one's way, finding one's path in the dark, or adjusting to unfavorable circumstances, possessing these abilities guarantees that hikers and survivalists can successfully manage any scenario, enhancing the safety and pleasure of their outdoor escapades.

THE END